Nelson Readers
Series editor: Lewis Jones

A library of graded readers for studen
reluctant native readers. The books ar
Structure, vocabulary, idiom and sent
principles laid down in detail in *A Tea
The books are listed below according
300 words and appropriate structures
words, 5: 2000 words and 6: 2500 wor
accompanied by a cassette.

GW01182464

Level One
Inspector Holt and the Fur Van* *John Tully*
Inspector Holt: Where is Bill Ojo? *John Tully*
Crocodile! *K R Cripwell*
Four Short Stories* *Margery Morris*
Fast Money *K R Cripwell*
It's a Trick! *Lewis Jones*
The Story of Macbeth *from Shakespeare*
Tin Lizzie* *Jane Homeshaw*
Dead in the Morning* *Jane Homeshaw*
Letters from the Dead* *Jane Homeshaw*
Taxi! *Jane Homeshaw*
The Pathfinders* *Jane Homeshaw*
Inspector Holt: Cats in the Dark* *John Tully*
Inspector Holt and the Chinese Necklace *John Tully*
Journey to Universe City *Leslie Dunkling*
Three Folk Tales* *Margaret Naudi*
The Man with Three Fingers* *John Tully*
Fastline UK *Jane Homeshaw*
The Grey Rider *Steve Rabley*
Love Me Tomorrow *Jane Homeshaw*
Dracula* *Bram Stoker*

Level Two
The Magic Garden *K R Cripwell*
Muhammed Ali: King of the Ring *John Tully*
Inspector Holt Gets His Man* *John Tully*
The Canterville Ghost* *Oscar Wilde*
The Prince and the Poor Boy *Mark Twain*
Inspector Holt: The Bridge* *John Tully*
Oliver Twist *Charles Dickens*
Two Roman Stories *from Shakespeare*
The Titanic is Sinking* *K R Cripwell*
Madame Tussaud's* *Lewis Jones*
Three Sherlock Holmes Adventures* *Sir Arthur Conan Doyle*
The Story of Scotland Yard *Lewis Jones*
The Charlie Chaplin Story* *Jane Homeshaw*
A King's Love Story *K R Cripwell*
Dangerous Earth *Jane Homeshaw*
Chariots of Fire* *W J Weatherby*
Shark Attack *Jan Keane*
The Complete Robot: Selected Stories *Isaac Asimov*
Roadie *Chris Banks*
The Mystery of Dr Fu Manchu *Sax Rohmer*
Michael Jackson: Who's Bad? *Jen Denniston*
Lord Arthur Savile's Crime *Oscar Wilde*

Level Three
Climb a Lonely Hill *Lilith Norman*
Custer's Gold *Kenneth Ulyatt*
Gunshot Grand Prix *Douglas Rutherford*
David Copperfield* *Charles Dickens*
Born Free *Joy Adamson*
Five Ghost Stories* *Viola Huggins*
Three English Kings *from Shakespeare*
An American Tragedy *Theodore Dreiser*
Six American Stories* *N Wymer*
Emma and I *Sheila Hocken*
Little Women *Louisa M Alcott*
The Picture of Dorian Gray* *Oscar Wilde*
Marilyn Monroe *Peter Dainty*
Bruce Springsteen *Toni Murphy*
Is That It? *Bob Geldof*
Short Stories *Oscar Wilde*
A Room with a View *E M Forster*
The Importance of Being Earnest *Oscar Wilde*
The Lost World *Sir Arthur Conan Doyle*
Arab Folk Tales *Helen Thomson*
Computers: From Beads to Bytes *Peter Dewar*
Treasure Island *Robert Louis Stevenson*
Nelson Mandela *Adrienne Swindells*

Level Four
The White South *Hammond Innes*
A Christmas Carol *Charles Dickens*
King Solomon's Mines*
H Rider Haggard
Jane Eyre *Charlotte Brontë*
Pride and Prejudice *Jane Austen*
Dr Jekyll and Mr Hyde*
R L Stevenson
Huckleberry Finn *Mark Twain*
Landslide *Desmond Bagley*
Nothing is the Number When You Die
Joan Fleming
The African Child *Camara Laye*
The Lovely Lady and Other Stories
D H Lawrence
Airport International *Brian Moynahan*
The Secret Sharer and other Sea Stories
Joseph Conrad
Death in Vienna? *K E Rowlands*
Hostage Tower* *Alistair MacLean*
The Potter's Wheel *Chukwuemeka Ike*
Tina Turner *Stephen Rabley*
Campbell's Kingdom *Hammond Innes*
Barchester Towers *Anthony Trollope*
Rear Window *Cornell Woolrich*
Britain: The Inside Story *Lewis Jones*

Level Five
The Guns of Navarone
Alistair MacLean
Geordie *David Walker*
Wuthering Heights *Emily Brontë*
Where Eagles Dare *Alistair MacLean*
Wreck of the Mary Deare
Hammond Innes
I Know My Love *Catherine Gaskin*
The Mayor of Casterbridge
Thomas Hardy
Sense and Sensibility *Jane Austen*
The Eagle Has Landed *Jack Higgins*
Middlemarch *George Eliot*
Victory *Joseph Conrad*
Experiences of Terror* *Roland John*
The Freedom Trap *Desmond Bagley*

Level Six
Doctor Zhivago *Boris Pasternak*
The Glory Boys *Gerald Seymour*
In the Shadow of Man *Jane Goodall*
Harry's Game *Gerald Seymour*
House of a Thousand Lanterns
Victoria Holt
Hard Times *Charles Dickens*
Sons and Lovers *D H Lawrence*
The Dark Frontier *Eric Ambler*
Vanity Fair *William Thackeray*
Inspector Ghote Breaks an Egg
H R F Keating

Nelson Readers Level 2

THE CHARLIE CHAPLIN STORY

Jane Homeshaw

Nelson

Thomas Nelson and Sons Ltd
Nelson House, Mayfield Road
Walton-on-Thames, Surrey
KT12 5PL, UK

51 York Place
Edinburgh
EH1 3JD, UK

Thomas Nelson (Hong Kong) Ltd
Toppan Building 10/F
22a Westlands Road
Quarry Bay, Hong Kong

© Jane Homeshaw 1983

First published by Collins ELT 1983

Reprinted: 1984, 1985, 1987 (twice), 1988 (twice), 1989 (twice)

ISBN 0-00-370150-6

This edition first published by
Thomas Nelson and Sons Ltd 1992

ISBN 0-17-556557-0
NPN 9 8 7 6 5 4 3 2
Cassette ISBN 0-17-556508-2

We are grateful to John Topham Picture Library for permission to reproduce the photograph which appears on the cover, and also the text photographs.
For permission to reproduce the photograph on page 42, we should like to thank Camera Press Ltd.
Cover design by Dan Lim.

All rights reserved. No part of this publication may be reproduced, copied or transmitted save with written permission or in accordance with the provisions of the Copyright, Design and Patents Act 1988, or under the terms of any licence permitting limited copying issued by the Copyright Licensing Agency, 90 Tottenham Court Road, London W1P 9HE.

Any person who does any unauthorised act in relation to this publication may be liable to criminal prosecution and civil claims for damages.

Printed in Great Britain
by Bell and Bain Ltd., Glasgow

Chapter One

The dancer finished her dance and began to sing. She had a sweet voice, but it wasn't very strong.

"Louder!" screamed the soldiers. "Sing louder!" The woman tried, but she couldn't. The soldiers began to laugh at her, and the woman stopped singing and started to cry.

Her five-year-old son stood a few metres from her. He wanted to help his mother, but he didn't know how. Suddenly a thought came to him. He jumped up beside her on the stage and called out: "I'll sing for you!"

The soldiers looked at the small child in front of them and laughed. But one soldier said: "Let him try. Let's listen to him."

The boy sang the song of Jack Jones, a London street-market seller. As he sang, he danced round the stage.

The soldiers loved it. They dropped money down on the stage. When the boy saw the money, he stopped singing and reached down for it.

"Sing!" the soldiers screamed.

"First I'll get the money, then I'll sing again," the boy called back. The soldiers laughed and more money rained down on the stage.

That night, the little boy and his mother took back to their home in Lambeth, South London, a lot of money. His mother never went on the stage again. But, in later years, Charlie Chaplin became a great star.

Chapter Two

"I'm not going to wear them!" Charlie eyed the red trousers in his mother's hands. "They're worse than Sydney's yellow shirt—and all the boys at school laughed at that!"

"You're right," said Sydney, Charlie's older brother.

"But you don't have any other trousers," cried his mother. "I made these with cloth from one of my old stage dresses. I worked on them all night."

"Why can't you buy me trousers in a shop?" said Charlie.

"You know why," said his mother. "We've no money." Now her days as a dancer and singer were over, and Hannah Chaplin's little family were very poor. Hannah tried to make dresses and sell them, but her eyes weren't very strong.

"Can't you ask Father?" said Sydney.

"I haven't seen your father for months," said Hannah. "He spends all his money on that woman. She lives with him now ... she and their child. If he doesn't spend his money on her, he spends it on drink. *I* don't see any of it."

"Sydney sells newspapers in the street," said Charlie. "But I'm only seven. What can I do to get some money?" He eyed the red trousers again.

He couldn't go to school in those. They were the trousers of ... of a dancer ...

"I know!" he said. "I'll go and sing and dance on the streets. Sydney will come with me, won't you, Sydney?"

"Of course," said Sydney. "And I'll wear my yellow shirt."

The boys often danced and sang on the streets of Lambeth after that, but they didn't make much money. They brought their pennies home to their mother. The pennies helped to buy a little food.

Hannah's eyes became worse. She couldn't see to cut the cloth for any more dresses. There was no food in the house at all.

People came from the Lambeth Town Office and took the boys away from her. They placed them in the Hanwell Schools for Poor Children. They put Charlie in one school and Sydney in another.

Charlie was very unhappy without his mother and brother. The teachers cut off his hair and the food was bad.

For a time, Hannah's eyes became better and the boys went home again. A clothes factory gave her cloth to make into dresses, so she could work at home. But after a time, she became sick and the doctors put her into hospital.

Sydney and Charlie went to live with their father and his other woman, Louise.

Louise wasn't happy about this. She didn't want the children of another woman in her house.

Their father was often away from home. He was a singer—but no famous theatre wanted him; he drank too much. Louise drank too. When she drank, she forgot about the children of 'that other woman.'

One night, eight-year-old Charlie came home and found the house empty. He couldn't get in, so he walked the streets for hours. At midnight, Louise came back, but she wouldn't let him in through the door.

When their father heard about it, he had a fight with Louise. But after that, things became worse for the boys. Louise often shut them out of the house.

As Charlie walked through London at night, he learned a lot about the poor people who lived and slept on the streets.

He never forgot these things.

After a while, Hannah came out of hospital. She found a room, and the clothes factory gave her work again. The boys came back to her and her husband gave her fifty pence a week.

One day Hannah saw an old man on the street. "Look at that old man, Charlie," she said. "His back is like the letter C. His eyes are on the road. When he walks, his feet never leave the ground. He walks like this ..."

Hannah got up from her chair and walked across the room. For a minute or two, she acted like the old man. She *was* the old man.

"Now you try," she told Charlie. Charlie tried it and found that he could act like the old man too.

Another day Hannah said: "Act like that cat, Charlie." Another day, it was a woman with a heavy bag.

One day, Charlie walked into the room and said: "Who am I?"

Hannah eyed him for a minute, then laughed. "That's easy," she said. "You're a young woman in love. You know, Charlie, you're a very good actor. I think you're ready to go on the stage."

Charlie became one of eight boys in *Eight Lancashire Lads*. They danced in theatres all over England. He got twelve and a half pence a week. But after a year, the job ended and Charlie went back home.

Chapter Three

The train came in and Sydney was on it. Charlie ran up to him.

"You're like a stranger in your seaman's clothes," Charlie told his brother. "Six months is a long time."

"You're right," said Sydney. He looked at his younger brother—the boy was dirty and his clothes were old and too big.

"How old are you now?" Sydney asked. "Eleven? You don't grow very fast. Why isn't mother here?"

"I've got something to tell you," said Charlie.

"All right," said Sydney. "There's a restaurant here. Would you like something to eat?"

"Yes please," said Charlie. "I haven't eaten since yesterday morning."

After the meal, Charlie said: "Mother went into hospital a month ago. The doctors think she'll never come out again."

"What did you do?" asked Sydney. "Did you go to Father?"

"He's dead," said Charlie. "The drink killed him in the end."

"But what did you do?" asked Sydney. "Did you get another job in a theatre?"

"In these clothes?" said Charlie. "No. I lived on the streets. I sold flowers for a time, and some woodcutters gave me a little food sometimes ..."

"Didn't you go to Lambeth Town Office? They helped us before."

"I didn't want to go back to Hanwell Schools," said Charlie. "Don't you remember? They cut off our hair before, and the older boys hurt us ... the teachers too, sometimes ... No. It was better to live on the streets."

"I've come home with twenty pounds," said Sydney. "I won't go to sea again. We'll get a room and some new clothes. Then we'll both go back on the stage."

In his new clothes, Charlie soon got a job in a theatre. He played a street newspaper-seller—a job from his real life. The real-life newspapers wrote about him. They called him 'a great child actor'. The play ran for three years in theatres all over the country.

Sydney didn't find a theatre job for a long time. But Charlie could now send him money. Their mother stayed in hospital. She was never well again.

During the next seven years, Charlie's work was his life. He had nothing else. On stage, he was often very funny, and people laughed. Off stage, he was always sad and alone.

Then Charlie fell in love.

"Please, Hetty! Please come out with me on Sunday."

Hetty's eyes were on the floor. She was only fifteen years old, but she was already a dancer. She wasn't ready to fall in love and marry. She didn't want to go out with this young man, but she was sorry for him.

"All right," she said.

Charlie couldn't believe his ears. He went to the bank and took out three pounds—a lot of money for him. He never liked to spend money. But Hetty must have the best.

On Sunday, he took Hetty in a taxi to one of London's most expensive restaurants—*The Trocadero*.

"What would you like to eat?" said Charlie. "You can have anything you want."

"I don't want anything," said Hetty. She was afraid to eat anything in this famous place.

"You must have *something*." said Charlie.

"I ... I had my supper before I came," said Hetty.

Charlie was also afraid in this place. He asked for too much food, then tried to eat it. While he ate and drank, he talked to Hetty about his love.

"You are as beautiful as the night," he told her. "I love your black hair and your dark eyes. I can never live without you ..."

Hetty became more afraid. She didn't want this man's love. She only wanted to go home ...

"Marry me!" said Charlie. "I shall die if you don't marry me!"

Hetty jumped up from the table. "I'm going home," she said. "Don't try to follow me."

After that evening, Hetty didn't want to speak to Charlie any more.

But Charlie never forgot Hetty Kelly. She was the first great love of his life. Her dark hair and dark eyes stayed with him all his life.

Chapter Four

Charlie wanted to leave England. Hetty didn't want him, and he knew that his mother would never leave hospital. England only brought him unhappiness. Perhaps America could give him a new start.

Fred Karno was a big name in the English theatre business. He looked for good, funny actors, and, when he found them, he sent them out to theatres in England, Europe and America.

Now Charlie went to him, and said: "I want to work in America."

Fred Karno looked at Charlie. "All right, Chaplin," he said. "I know you're a good actor. You worked for me before. Now listen. I've got a good act called *The Wow-Wows*. They're going to America soon. They're going to play in theatres all over the country. You can go with them. I'll pay you fifteen pounds a week."

The Americans didn't like *The Wow-Wows*. In one part of their act, Charlie came on stage with an empty teacup. He asked for some water.

"Why do you want water?"

"I want to have a bath."

In England, people thought this was funny. But

the New Yorkers didn't laugh. Perhaps the English always had a bath in a teacup?

Charlie began to look at American funny acts. What did they do to be funny? He saw that they were much faster. They spoke faster and they ran round the stage more. They often fell down and had a lot of 'fights'. Charlie started to change his act.

An American theatre newspaper wrote about *The Wow-Wows*. It didn't like the act, but it said about Charlie: 'There was one funny Englishman ... and he will do well in America.'

The Wow-Wows left New York and started to work in theatres all over America. They played in Chicago, Minneapolis, St. Louis, Kansas City, San Francisco and Los Angeles. The Americans

Charlie (in the lifebelt) on his way to America

in these cities still didn't like *The Wow-Wows*. But some of them thought Charlie Chaplin was funny.

In Los Angeles, Charlie walked round the streets with one of the other actors. They looked at the tall, new buildings, and at the big, open streets.

"It's very different from England," said the other actor.

"Yes," said Charlie. "I like it. I like the people."

"But there are poor people here, the same as in England."

"But they work hard here," said Charlie. "And if they work hard, they can make a lot of money."

"*You* like the thought of that, Charlie," smiled the other actor.

They passed a cinema. Hundreds of people waited for the doors to open.

"Why do they want to see these new films? Why don't they come to our theatre to see us?"

"One day soon, the cinema is going to take the place of the theatre," Charlie told him.

"Never. I don't believe that."

"It's true," Chaplin said. "And I want to be a part of it, if I can. But I don't see how it can happen. We're going back to New York for six weeks, and after that we'll leave for England."

A few weeks later, in New York, a young man named Mack Sennet went to the theatre with a friend. Mack worked as a small-part actor in the new film business. He got five dollars a day.

He turned to his friend in the seat beside him and said: "If I ever become a big film-maker, I want that man in one of my films."

"What man?"

"That funny little man with the black hair. What's his name? ... ... Charlie Chaffin."

A few days later, Charlie got on a boat back to England.

In 1913, Charlie was back in America. A telegram came to the theatre. It said: '*Do you have an actor named Chaffin?*'

The telegram came from Mack Sennet who was now a film-maker in Los Angeles. Mack remembered the little Englishman and he wanted to help him to be a star.

In the year 1912-1913, Mack Sennet made a hundred and forty films and a million dollars. The films were short—a few minutes long—and, of course, there was no sound. The actors didn't talk: they moved fast.

They jumped in front of trains or cars—real ones. They fell downstairs or fought on top of buses. They were ready to do anything—anything that would bring laughs.

Some of Sennet's actors played funny policemen, called *The Keystone Cops*. They were mostly young. He found them all over America and brought them to Los Angeles.

Now Sennet found Charlie, and wanted him there too.

Charlie was afraid. It was his third day in Los Angeles, and he was afraid to walk into the *Keystone Film Studios*.

Every morning, he took a streetcar from his hotel and went and stood outside. He saw the actors come out at lunchtime and cross the road to the foodshop. But he was afraid to go inside.

On the third day, like the other days, he went back to his hotel. He sat on the bed and thought: "Charlie, you'll never be a filmstar. Go back to the theatre where you belong."

The sound of the telephone cut through his thoughts. "Hi! Mack Sennet here. We're waiting for you at the Studios." So Charlie left the hotel.

Mr Sennet was pleased to see Charlie, and took him to one of the studios.

It was in the open air, but a soft white light shone down on the stage. It came from the sun that shone through long white pieces of cloth high above his head.

In 1913, film-makers used only sunlight. That was why they made films in California. There were long hours of sunlight all through the year.

"Look round for a few days, Charlie," said Mr Sennet. "Learn something about the film business."

On that first day, Charlie learned that they made two or three films on the same stage at the same time. The film studios made two or three films a week.

A door stood in the middle of one part of the stage. The famous filmstar, Miss Mabel Normand, stood and banged on the door with her hand.

The cameramen filmed this again and again. Then they stopped their cameras and took them to another part of the stage. In this way, Charlie learned that people made films in little bits. At the end of two or three days, Sennet put together the best bits to make one piece of film.

Nine days passed before Charlie got a part in his first film. He worked for Henry Lehrman.

Charlie worked hard and put in a lot of funny 'business'. In three days, the film was ready for the cinemas. When he saw the film, he wanted to cry. His funny business was not in the film.

In later years, Henry Lehrman said: "I thought Charlie knew too much for a beginner."

The next day, Mack Sennet called Charlie.

"Go and put on some clothes — any clothes

— and do something funny to your face. I want you in this next film."

So Charlie looked for some clothes. He found some trousers that were too big for him, a coat that was too small, some shoes that were too big and a hat that was too small. He put them all on and looked at himself in the glass.

He walked up and down the room and put his feet out to either side.

He looked at his face in the glass again. He took off his hat, closed one eye and opened it, then dropped his hat on his head again.

The man in the glass wasn't Charlie now. He was a different person. A man without money but rich in happiness. A man who wanted to do the right thing—but who was always wrong. A great lover—but no woman ever loved him.

But he still wanted something else ... of course!

Charlie cut a short piece of black hair and placed it under his nose. That was it—a small moustache.

When he walked onto the studio floor, Mack Sennet couldn't stop laughing.

"Wh ... who are you?" he screamed.

The Tramp — a man without money but rich in happiness

Charlie said: "This man is always looking for love and adventure, but he runs away from any danger. He wants you to believe that he is a scientist, a sportsman, a millionaire, a leader of men ... but he's always alone and he never has any money. He's a tramp who lives on the streets. He'll use cigarettes after people drop them on the street. He'll take chocolate from a baby. And, of course, he'll kick a lady—but only when he's unhappy."

"OK," said Sennet. "Let's see. Start the cameras."

The story of the film was about an hotel. The little tramp came through its doors. He fell over a lady's foot and took off his hat to her. Then he turned round and fell over a chair. He took off his hat to that, too ...

Actors, cameramen, cleaners—they all came to look at Sennet's new filmstar—and they stayed to laugh.

Mack Sennet used twenty-three metres of film on Charlie's funny business that afternoon. In most films, funny business used about three metres.

"It's too long," said Sennet.

"If it's funny, it can't be too long," Charlie answered.

Charlie went home on the streetcar with a man who told him: "Boy, you started something today. No actor ever got those kind of laughs before."

"Let's hope they laugh in the same way in the cinemas," said Charlie.

They did. And they went on laughing at The Tramp for forty years.

Chapter Five

In his year with Mack Sennet, Charlie made a lot of films and worked hard—perhaps too hard. He became afraid that people would get tired of his films. How long would Americans go on laughing at him?

Charlie wanted to make a lot of money in a very short time. He never forgot the bad days when he was a child.

He told Mack Sennet: "I want a thousand dollars a week."

"But I don't get that," said Sennet.

"The people don't stand outside the cinemas to see *you*."

"I can't give you a thousand a week," said Sennet.

"I'm sorry," said Chaplin, "But I'll have to leave you."

Charlie next went to make films for the *Essanay Company*, but he wasn't happy with them either.

Charlie's brother Sydney was now in America. He was good with money and he acted as Charlie's business man.

"You're getting only 1250 dollars a week. It isn't enough," he told Charlie. "*Essanay* are making millions of dollars out of your films."

The brothers asked for more money, but *Essanay* said no.

Sydney told Charlie: "I'm going to New York. That's where the money is. You come too when you finish this film."

So Charlie finished the film, and got on a train to New York. Before he left, he sent Sydney a telegram—'*Leaving Los Angeles tonight. Will reach New York in five days.*'

Just before the train arrived in Amarillo—the first stop after Los Angeles—Charlie went to the bathroom for a wash. At the station there was a lot of noise. Undressed, and with soap on his face, he looked out of the window.

Thousands of people were out there—and tables with a lot of food and drink on them.

"Must be for some Mr Big," thought Charlie. He put more soap on his face. Then he heard voices.

"Where is he? Where's Charlie Chaplin?"

The people wanted him. They wanted to say thank you. Thank you for making us laugh.

Back on the train, Charlie got more telegrams:

'*Charlie. We're waiting for you in Kansas City.*'

'*When you arrive in Chicago, a car will be ready for you.*'

'*Come and stay with us in the Blackstone Hotel.*'

All the way to New York, people stood on

stations, in fields, on the roads. They held up their hands as the train passed.

The poor little boy from South London was a star.

Sydney did good business in New York. With his help, Charlie got 670 000 dollars a year. He was still only twenty-seven.

He loved his work. He made one film every month. *The Floor Walker, The Fireman, Easy Street* and *The Adventurer* were some of these.

In later years, Charlie looked back on this year as the happiest time of his life. In his films, he was still The Tramp, but in real life he was nearly a millionaire.

His mother came over from England. She was still sick, but there was a beautiful house by the sea, with doctors and other people to help her.

She was never well again, but her sons tried hard to bring happiness to her last years.

Chapter Six

Charlie never forgot his first love, Hetty Kelly, the fifteen-year-old London dancer. All his life, in his mind, a beautiful woman was always a very young girl, with Hetty's dark hair and dark eyes.

At the end of 1917, he married sixteen-year-old Mildred Harris. She was dark and beautiful but Charlie wasn't happy with her for long. He couldn't talk to her.

After the end of his marriage, Charlie worked hard on his films. One of his most famous films was *The Kid*. He made the film with Jackie Coogan, the child actor.

Chaplin said: "They say babies and dogs make the best actors in films. Put a twelve-month-old baby into a bath with a piece of soap and all the world will laugh."

After *The Kid*, he made another film about a tramp without money who wants to go on holiday. Like the rich, he goes south to find the sun. Like the rich, he goes by train—but *under* the train and without a ticket.

When he finished making this film (*The Idle Class*), Charlie was very tired. Tired and alone. He tried to make another film, but he stopped in the middle of it because a letter came for him. It was from Hetty Kelly. She wrote:

'Do you remember a girl called Hetty? I'm married now, and I live in Portman Square. If you ever come to London, please come and see me.'

Charlie bought a ticket on a boat for England.

In England, the newspapers were full of pieces about Charlie. *'This little man with his funny feet.'* *'An army of people are waiting to say hello to The Tramp.'* *'Our Charlie is coming home.'* *'All London talks of Chaplin's visit.'*

The front page of one newspaper held only two words—*'OUR SON'*.

Charlie comes home; everyone wants to say hello

But one person didn't wait for Charlie. When he arrived in Southampton, Arthur Kelly, Hetty's brother, was there to meet him.

"Hetty died, you know," he said.

Charlie walked round the London streets. He visited Kennington Gate, where he met Hetty on that Sunday evening. But she didn't come to meet him now.

Unhappy, he crossed over from England to France. Still unhappy, he went to Germany, then back to Paris. In the end, he went back to America—to his work.

His next film was *A Woman of Paris*. It wasn't a funny film—it was a film about love. For the first time, the Americans didn't like a Charlie Chaplin film.

Chaplin next made *The Gold Rush*—perhaps his greatest film. He looked for an actress to play the girl.

He found Lita Grey—fifteen, dark-haired and dark-eyed—and he married her. Soon she had a baby, so Charlie got another actress for his film. In two years, Lita had two children, but before the year 1926 ended, their marriage ended too. Charlie fell in love with Lita's beauty—really it was Hetty Kelly's beauty. Once again, as with

Chaplin in one of his best films – The Gold Rush

Mildred Harris, he found he couldn't talk to a fifteen-year-old girl. But by that time, it was too late.

Like a farmer with a good cow, Lita milked Charlie for a lot of money. And she gave stories to the newspapers about their marriage.

From this time, the newspapers began to write against Chaplin.

Chapter Seven

Something else happened in the film business about this time. People began to use sound in films. Actors not only moved—they also talked.

This was bad news for Charlie. His kind of story was better without words.

Take a piece from one of his films:

The tramp is sitting in a restaurant. A man at a table smiles at him. The tramp smiles back. It happens again, and the tramp smiles again. He can't understand why the man is smiling, but the tramp wants to be friendly—he doesn't have many friends.

Then the tramp turns round and he does understand—there's a pretty girl behind him.

Chaplin made another film—*City Lights*. He gave it music, but the actors didn't speak. The film made a lot of money, but Charlie knew he must make a talking picture soon, or people would forget him.

People always want new things—new clothes, new films, new machines. People want change—but Charlie wasn't very happy about it.

Chaplin in the film, City Lights – *he gave it music*

"This is going to be a film about the future," Charlie told dark-haired Paulette Goddard. "And you are going to star in it with me. You must learn to dance and sing."

"All right," said Paulette.

"I'm going to call it *Modern Times*," said Charlie. "It's a film about the unkind future—a future where machines do the work of men."

"Is it going to be a talking picture?" asked Paulette.

Modern Times – *'a film about the future'*

"No," said Charlie. "There'll be a lot of machine noises. There'll be music and dancing, but no words. You and I will be the two tramps who try to live in this unkind world. But, at the end of the film, we'll walk away from the modern city. We'll walk down the road and out into the country with green fields and trees. And then, Paulette, I want to marry you."

Charlie and Paulette went away on holiday after the film, and they got married. But in 1940, Paulette walked out of his life.

Europe was at war, but America wasn't yet a part of it. In 1941, Britain stood alone against Germany. Then, Russia changed sides and became Britain's friend.

Charlie wanted America to help Britain and Russia. He spoke at meetings round the country and said: "We must help our Russian friends who are fighting a war against our enemies."

A lot of Americans didn't like that. They began to turn away from him. He didn't make talking pictures. He wasn't married to Paulette Goddard any more. And there were worse things—wasn't his name (with the names of other women) on the front pages of newspapers every day?

In the middle of it all, he met and married Oona O'Neill. She was dark-haired, dark-eyed and beautiful; the daughter of Eugene O'Neill, a

Charlie with his beautiful young wife, Oona

writer of famous plays. The newspapers didn't like it. Charlie was fifty-four, and Oona was only eighteen.

In 1942, Japan made war on America, so America fought back on the side of Russia and Britain.

But after the war, America was still afraid of Russia. A lot of people thought there were perhaps Russian spies in America. Their eyes fell on filmstars and writers—Charlie Chaplin was one of them.

Wasn't it true that, before and during the war, Charlie spoke kindly about Russia? Wasn't it true that Charlie wasn't an American? They remembered his words: "We must help our Russian friends."

Yes. Chaplin must be an enemy of the American way of life.

Charlie tried to talk to them.

"I love this country. It's my home. I came to America when I was poor and without friends. America has given me everything. I'm famous because I'm one of your filmstars. I'm rich because you let me work hard. I married Oona, an American woman. My children are American."

But they answered with another question.

"Do you like the Russians?"

Charlie said: "In American, aren't I free to like Russia—or any other country?"

Chapter Eight

Charlie made his last great film—*Limelight*. It was about an old actor who falls in love with a beautiful young dancer. She wants to die because she's afraid she can't dance any more. The old man stops her. He talks to her and tells her that life is beautiful. She listens to him, tries again, and becomes famous.

At the end of the film, the old actor dies because people don't think he's funny any more.

When he finished *Limelight*, Charlie was very tired.

"Let's take the children and go on holiday to Europe," said Oona.

Charlie smiled at Oona and said: "You always know what's best for me, my love. It was a happy day when I met you."

On the ship, in mid-Atlantic, Charlie got a telegram. It told him that the United States of America didn't want him back in their country.

"If America doesn't want us, we'll live in Europe," said Oona.

"America will have *you* back Oona. *You're* an American."

"If they don't want you, they won't get me back either," Oona answered.

Charlie and Oona in London; America didn't want him

Charlie spent the last twenty-five years of his life in Switzerland.

But in 1972, when he was eighty-two, America asked Charlie to come back. He went for a short visit. Thousands of people in New York stood and screamed their happiness—their love for the great old man.

And, in Hollywood, they gave him an Oscar—the film world's biggest 'thank you' to any actor.

So at the end of his life, America said, "We're sorry, Charlie, about the past. You've done great things for us. Thank you."

Charlie Chaplin aged 85

Charlie Chaplin died on December 25th 1977. His wife, Oona, was at his bedside. Oona was Charlie's last love. They stayed together for 33 years—for life—and they had eight children. That was another happy ending for Charlie.

Four of the children of Charlie and Oona

A Word Game

Find the right letter in each line and put it in the box. You can read down the answer when you have found all eleven letters.

My first is in tea, but not in sea. ☐
My second's in he, but not in me. ☐
My third is in head, but not in had. ☐
My fourth is in bag, but not in bad. ☐
My fifth is in does, but not in dies. ☐
My sixth is in yells, but not in eyes. ☐
My seventh's in bed, but not in be. ☐
My eighth is in ear, but not in tea. ☐
My ninth is in use, but not in set. ☐
My tenth is in seat, but not in ate. ☐
My eleventh's in she, but not in west. ☐

This film was, perhaps, one of Chaplin's best.

A Crossword

Do you like crosswords? Here's one for you. Find the answers to the questions. Then write the answers in the boxes. Some of the answers go *across* from left to right. And some of them go *down* the page.

Across

1. You go to see actors in this building. (7)
2. Birds fly through the _____. (3)
3. In most of his films, Charlie dressed like one of these. (5)
4. Not hers. (3)
5. '... some woodcutters gave _____ a little food sometimes ...' (2)
6. 'When the boy saw the money, he stopped singing and _____ down for it.' (7)

Down

1. Worker in a school. (7)
5. Not you. (2)
7. Hetty was afraid to _____ anything in the Trocadero restaurant. (3)
8. You can find boats and ships on this. (3)
9. The same word as 2 across. (3)
10. Charlie took a _____ from Los Angeles to New York. (5)
11. Dip time? Wrong! He didn't *fill* the cup. He _____ it. (7)

Answer to the Word Game

The Gold Rush

Answers to the Crossword

Across

1. theatre   2. air   3. tramp   4. his   5. me
6. reached

Down

1. teacher   5. me   7. eat   8. sea   9. air
10. train   11. emptied

Now you can read

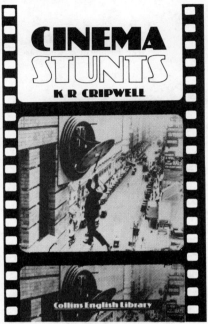

Cinema Stunts at Level 3

Find out how James Bond jumps over a police car in his racing boat in the film, *Live and Let Die*. Learn the secrets of the men and women in films who fall under running horses, hang from planes on ropes and die in burning houses.

This book describes and explains some of the most exciting stunts in the cinema.